AF286821

RESISTANCE IS FUTILE

THE ULTIMATE GUIDE TO IDENTIFYING RESISTANCE TO CHANGE

BY OSCAR BERG

CREATED BY OSCAR BERG
oscarberg.net

ILLUSTRATIONS BY LEREMY GAN
leremy.com

PUBLISHER: Gr8 Mountains AB, Lund, Sweden
PRINT: Books on Demand GmbH, Germany
ISBN: 978-91-988416-1-9

INTRODUCTION

Resistance to change arises when we, as individuals or organizations, oppose new initiatives or changes. Often it is driven by fear of the unknown, wanting to stay in our comfort zone, or not understanding the benefits of change.

Much of it stems from various cognitive bias that means we, as individuals or groups, prefer the status quo. We perceive losses as more painful than we view gains as positive. We also naturally value immediate rewards over future rewards. When we're tired, we'd rather eat chocolate that instantly perks us up than consistently exercise to feel better in the long run.

Our inclination to stick to the familiar and avoid unnecessary change can be traced back to our evolutionary biology. Our brains are optimized to minimize effort and maximize reward. In the past, in a world where resources were scarce and our survival uncertain, it was advantageous to avoid risks and conserve our physical and cognitive resources. In other words, it's in our nature to resist change. Paradoxically, even when it's necessary to improve our situation.

To make better decisions and create a brighter future for ourselves and the organizations we're part of, we must become aware of our resistance behaviors. Then we can work on understanding and addressing the reasons behind them. Perhaps we need to communicate better about ongoing change? Address concerns and fears? Provide support and resources? Or tailor change to make it more acceptable?

My aim with this book is to highlight standard resistance behaviors, both organizational and individual. By understanding and laughing at it all, rather than criticizing or punishing people for behaving this way, I believe we can foster a more open and supportive work culture. A work culture where people feel free to express their concerns and collaborate to find solutions.

'The greatest danger in times of turbulence is not the turbulence, it's acting with yesterday's logic.'

— Peter F. Drucker

HOW TO RESIST CHANGE AS AN ORGANIZATION

IGNORE THE CHANGE

AVOID INFORMATION THAT MIGHT BE BAD NEWS, SUCH AS THE NEED FOR ORGANIZATIONAL CHANGE.

NO HURRY!

CONVINCE YOURSELF THERE'S NO HURRY TO IMPLEMENT ANY
CHANGES. IT'S BEST TO WAIT AND SEE WHAT OTHERS DO.

'Doing more of what doesn't work won't make it work any better.'

— Charles Gibbons, Canadian abstract artist

CARRY ON AS USUAL

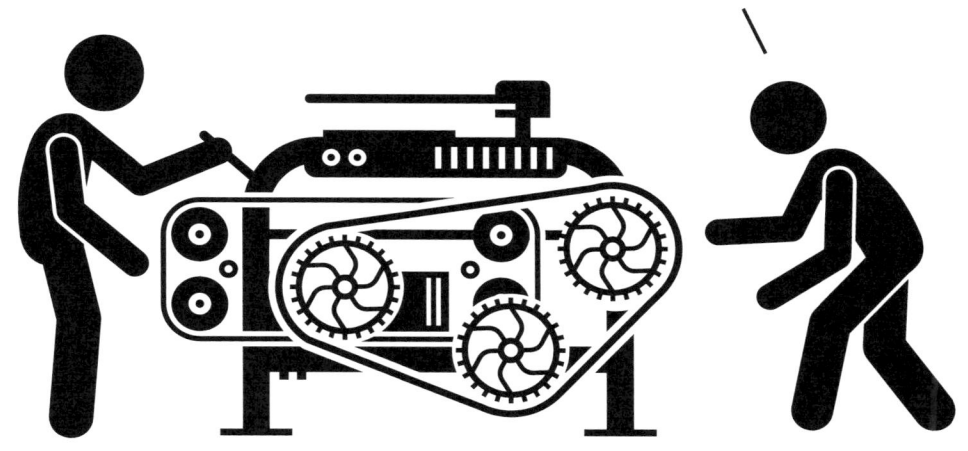

Try again! Next time, perhaps the machine will produce a mobile phone instead of a piece of metal as it's designed to.

KEEP ON DOING WHAT YOU'VE ALWAYS DONE. CLING TO THE HOPE IT WILL LEAD TO SOMETHING NEW THAT PLEASES THE MARKET AND OTHER STAKEHOLDERS.

REORGANIZE

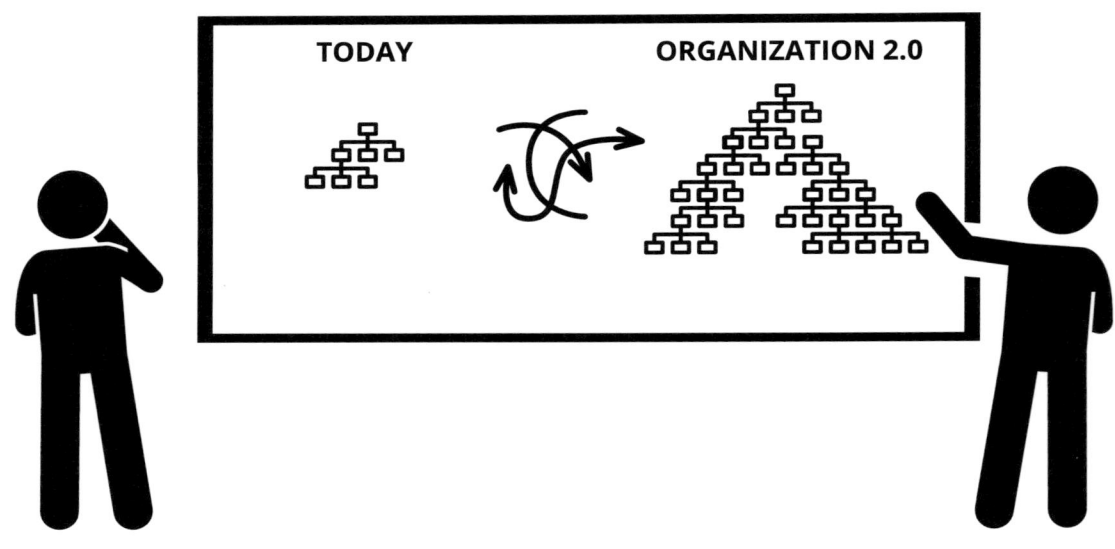

IMPLEMENT A REORGANIZATION THAT DRAWS ATTENTION TO STRUCTURAL CHANGES. THAT WAY YOU CAN AVOID MAKING ANY SUBSTANTIAL CHANGES.

MAKE THE NUMBERS LOOK GOOD

COMMIT TO CREATIVE ACCOUNTING. INFLATE ASSETS THAT ARE ESSENTIALLY WORTHLESS, SUCH AS A BRAND WEIGHED DOWN BY TRADITION.

LAUNCH A CHANGE PROGRAM

PUT TOGETHER A LARGE TEAM TO DEVELOP AMBITIOUS
PLANS THAT NEVER LEAVE THEIR CONFIDENTIAL
'STRATEGY ROOM'.

HIRE PREMIUM CONSULTANTS

PAY HEFTY SUMS TO EXPENSIVE CONSULTANTS. THE CHANGE INITIATIVE IS PRACTICALLY GUARANTEED TO FAIL AND WILL BE ABANDONED IN A COUPLE OF YEARS.

PICK A GOOD KPI

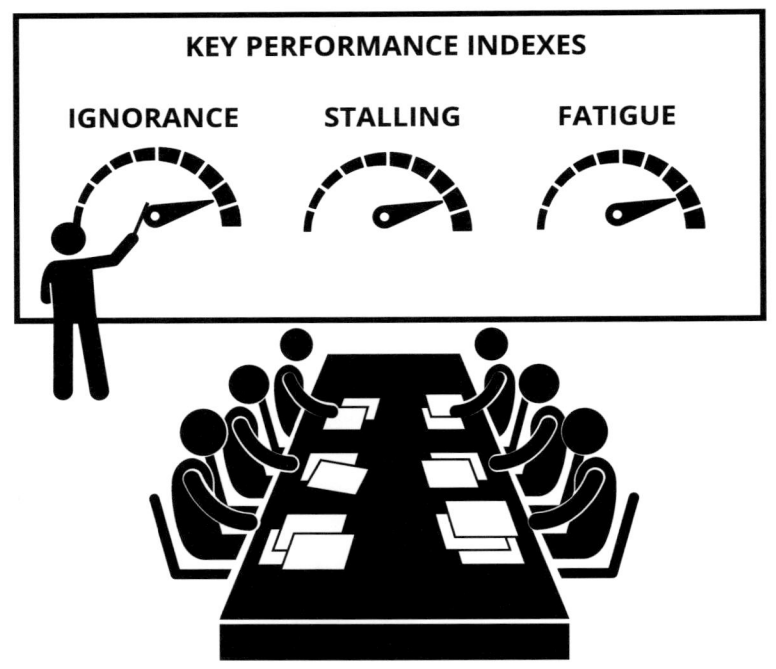

IMPLEMENT NEW PERFORMANCE MEASUREMENT METHODS THAT YOU CAN MEET NO MATTER WHAT.

PUT YOUR FAITH IN MODERN TECH

INITIATE AN AI PROJECT DESIGNED TO DEVELOP AN AI SOLUTION. IT WILL ADDRESS ALL YOUR CHALLENGES IN A FEW YEARS.

REVITALIZE THE BRAND

LAUNCH A FRESH NEW LOGO AND A GRAPHIC IDENTITY THAT FEELS SUPER MODERN AND COOL. NO OTHER CHANGES ARE NEEDED AS A RESULT.

CHANGE THE NARRATIVE

We aren't focused on profit; our mission is to better the world!

ALTER YOUR PUBLIC NARRATIVE ABOUT WHY YOUR ORGANIZATION EXISTS SO IT'S MORE VISIONARY AND MEANINGFUL.

IF IT WORKS DON'T FIX IT

THERE'S NO NEED TO MAKE CHANGES UNLESS THERE'S AN OBVIOUS ISSUE.

WAIT UNTIL NEXT YEAR

Change is like fashion, with new trends emerging every year. Trying to keep pace can often seem futile.

IT'S NOT WORTH MAKING CHANGES IF THERE WILL BE NEW CHANGES NEXT YEAR THAT WILL REQUIRE US TO REVISE EVERYTHING AGAIN.

'Faced with the choice between changing one's mind and proving that there is no need to do so, almost everyone gets busy on the proof.'

— Ken Galbraith,
Canadian American economist and diplomat

LOOK FOR COUNTER-EVIDENCE

EVEN THE SMALLEST PIECE OF EVIDENCE CAN CHALLENGE THE NOTION THAT YOUR ORGANIZATION NEEDS TO CHANGE.

INVENT NEW ROLES

Chief Transformation Officer

CREATE NEW ROLES TO GIVE THE ILLUSION OF CHANGE, AND THEN BLAME THEM WHEN THERE'S NO REAL CHANGE.

CREATE 'TEMPORARY' SOLUTIONS

ADDRESS ISSUES WITH 'TEMPORARY' SOLUTIONS TO DELAY GENUINE CHANGE.

CREATE A DISTRACTION

YOUR BEST DISTRACTIONS AND DIVERSIONARY TACTICS
WILL KEEP THE MARKET AND STAKEHOLDERS OBLIVIOUS
TO THE NEED FOR CHANGE.

HOLD FOCUS GROUPS

ENDLESS FOCUS GROUPS WILL CREATE THE IMPRESSION
THAT YOU'RE EARNESTLY TACKLING THE NEED FOR CHANGE.

PINPOINT THE ROOT CAUSE

SINGLE OUT A SINGLE INDIVIDUAL AS THE ROOT OF ALL YOUR BUSINESS CHALLENGES.

CREATE A REALITY DISTORTION FIELD

DISTORT EVERYONE'S PERCEPTION OF REALITY TO ALIGN
WITH YOUR DESIRED NARRATIVE.

ADOPT COOL NEW METHODS

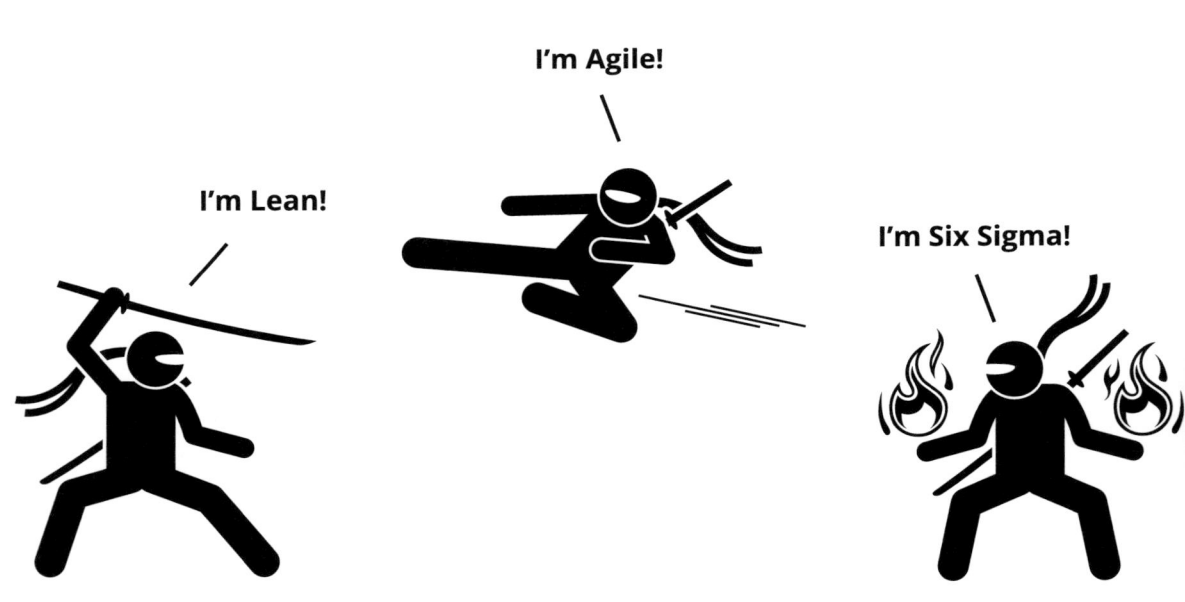

INVEST ALL YOUR TIME, ENERGY, AND RESOURCES IN ADOPTING WORKING METHODS THAT DIVERT ATTENTION FROM THOSE URGENT CHANGES.

HIDE THE BAD PARTS

LIMIT TRANSPARENCY WITHIN THE BUSINESS TO OBSCURE
ITS UNDERPERFORMANCE. HIDE ALL LOSSES AND
UNDERPERFORMING ASSETS IN AN OBSCURE SUBSIDIARY.

BOOST EXECUTIVE BONUSES

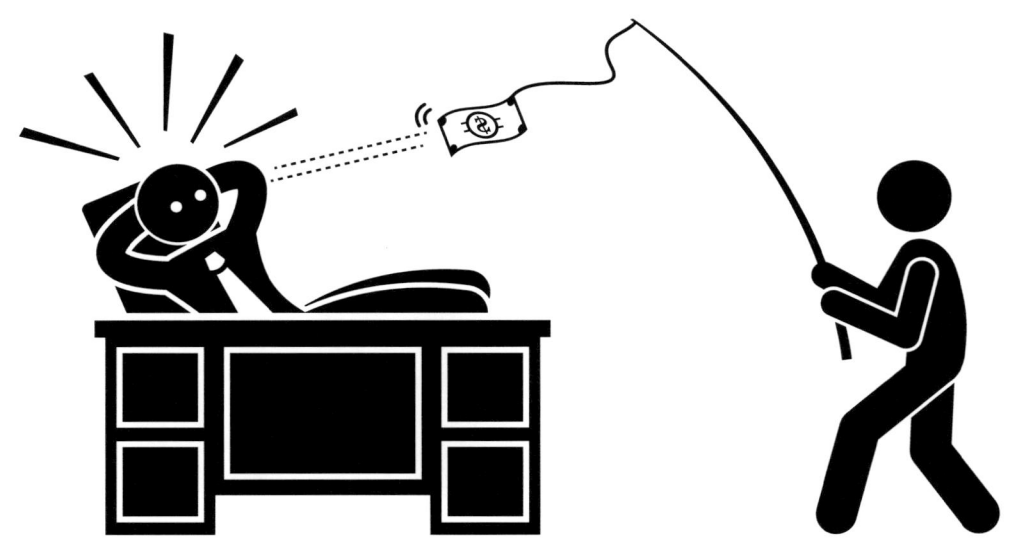

BOOST THE BONUSES FOR TOP EXECUTIVES. SURELY
EVERYTHING WILL BE FINE IF THOSE MOST RESPONSIBLE
FOR THE ISSUES ARE PAID MORE.

MIGRATE TO THE CLOUD

MIGRATE ALL YOUR IT SYSTEMS TO THE CLOUD AND NO ONE WILL DOUBT YOUR READINESS FOR THE FUTURE.

BEFRIEND STARTUPS

PARTNER WITH TRENDY STARTUPS AND PEOPLE WILL
OVERLOOK YOUR PROFITABILITY AND WON'T ASK
IF YOUR BUSINESS MODEL IS VIABLE.

LAUNCH AN APP!

The company has been saved! This app, which allows tracking of our stock price, will be a true game-changer!

LAUNCH AN APP AND YOU'RE GOOD TO GO! NO OTHER CHANGES REQUIRED.

JUST WORK HARDER

WORK FASTER, WORK LONGER DAYS, SKIP BREAKS. THAT IS GUARANTEED TO FIX EVERYTHING.

FORM COMMITTEES

SET UP COMMITTEES AND DIRECT ALL CHANGE-RELATED INQUIRIES TO THEM FOR 'IN-DEPTH ANALYSIS AND CONSIDERATION'.

DO AS YOU'VE ALWAYS DONE

DEMONSTRATE THAT THE METHODS, PROCESSES, OR MINDSETS YOU'VE CONSISTENTLY RELIED ON ARE STILL EFFECTIVE.

TAKE PRIDE IN TRADITION

This approach is a cherished tradition of ours, dating back to before the construction of the pyramids.

Weren't they using logs to move the stone blocks?"

TAKE PRIDE IN STICKING TO YOUR TRADITIONS AND WORKING METHODS, WHICH HAVE REMAINED LARGELY UNCHANGED SINCE THE COMPANY WAS FOUNDED.

INFLUENCE PUBLIC OPINION

DO WHAT YOU CAN TO SHAPE PUBLIC OPINION IN FAVOR OF EVERYTHING POSITIVE FOR YOUR COMPANY. AND OF COURSE, AGAINST EVERYTHING THAT MIGHT BE NEGATIVE.

HOST INNOVATION CONTESTS

HOST INNOVATION CONTESTS FOR ANONYMOUS
IMPROVEMENT SUGGESTIONS, WITHOUT A SYSTEM
TO IMPLEMENT THE IDEAS.

RETURN TO THE OFFICE

BLAME ALL YOUR PROBLEMS ON REMOTE WORKING. ORDER ALL EMPLOYEES BACK TO THE OFFICE SO YOU BECOME MORE PRODUCTIVE AND INNOVATIVE.

LET'S DRINK TO EVERY FAILURE!

EMBRACE THE IDEA THAT FAILURES ARE LEARNING
OPPORTUNITIES AND THUS THE PATH TO SUCCESS. SO WHEN
YOU FAIL, IT'S SOMETHING TO CELEBRATE!

PARTY LIKE IT'S 1999!

THE COMPANY IS ON THE SKIDS ANYWAY, SO WHY NOT JUST KICK BACK AND PARTY? BEATS CRYING IN THE SHOWER OVERWHELMED BY DREAD AND ANXIETY, RIGHT?

BLAME YOUR TECH

JUST BLAME IT ON THE TECH. AFTER ALL, IT'S THE SIMPLEST
WAY TO TURN A BLIND EYE TO THE ACTUAL ISSUES AND
DODGE FIXING THEM.

'I think there's a world market for maybe five computers.'

— Thomas Watson, chairman of IBM, 1943

BE YOUR OWN FORTUNE TELLER

CRAFT YOUR OWN FORECASTS THAT FAVOR THE COMPANY, CONVENIENTLY OVERLOOKING ANY FORM OF PROGRESSION OR CHANGE.

SET UP AN INNOVATION LAB

How cool is it that my company established its innovation lab on the moon?

CREATE AN ISOLATED INNOVATION LAB THAT CAN WORK ON INNOVATION INDEPENDENTLY WITHOUT AFFECTING THE MAIN BUSINESS.

TALK, TALK, TALK...

Blah blah blah blah blah blah blah blah blah blah blah blah blah blah
blah blah blah blah blah blah blah blah blah blah blah blah blah blah
blah blah blah blah blah blah blah blah blah blah blah blah blah blah
blah blah blah blah blah blah blah blah blah blah blah blah blah blah
blah blah blah blah blah blah blah blah blah blah blah blah blah blah
blah blah blah blah blah blah blah blah blah blah blah blah blah blah
blah blah blah blah blah blah blah blah blah blah blah blah blah blah
blah blah blah blah blah blah blah blah blah blah blah blah blah blah
blah blah blah blah blah blah blah blah blah blah blah blah blah blah

DISCUSS ABOUTE EVERYTHING THAT NEEDS TO BE DONE FOR HOURS ON END. SOON IT'LL FEEL LIKE YOU'VE ACHIEVED WHAT YOU'VE MERELY TALKED ABOUT.

ATTEND COOL EVENTS

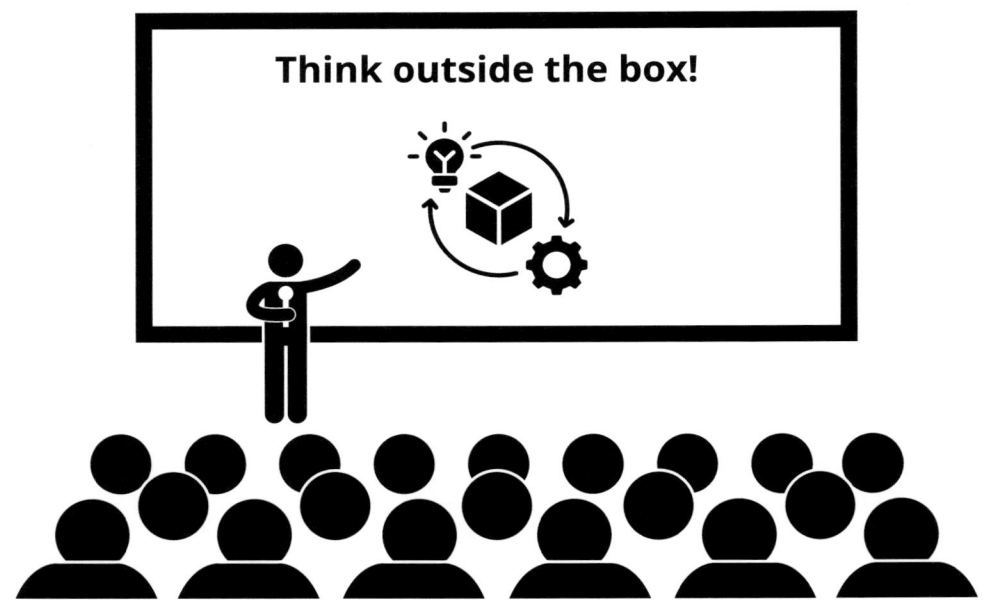

ATTEND INSPIRATIONAL LECTURES WITH INNOVATION GURUS TO LEARN BUZZWORDS YOU CAN USE INSTEAD OF IMPLEMENTING REAL CHANGE.

LEAD BY OPINION

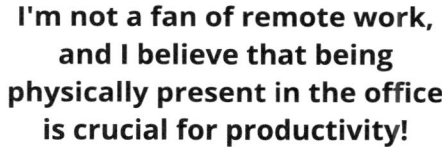

We've noticed an increase in productivity when our employees have the flexibility to choose where they work.

I'm not a fan of remote work, and I believe that being physically present in the office is crucial for productivity!

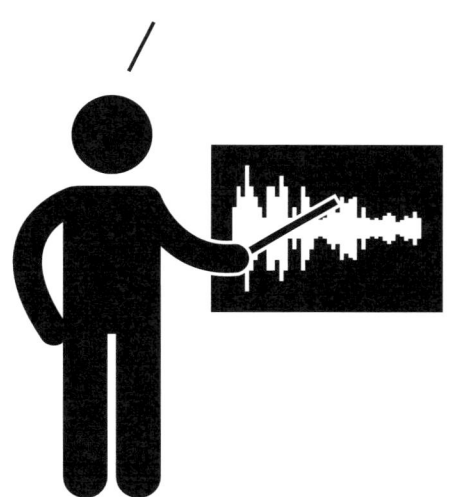

EMPLOY A CEO WHO PRIORITIZES PERSONAL OPINIONS OVER FACTS, ENABLING THEM TO IGNORE ANY SIGNS THAT THE COMPANY NEEDS TO EVOLVE.

RANDOM LAYOFFS

..and your position is being terminated because your name begins with a 'B' and is three letters long.

APPEASE THE MARKET AND CREATE AN ILLUSION OF MEANINGFUL TRANSFORMATION BY LAYING PEOPLE OFF ARBITRARILY.

SMEAR THE COMPETITION

SMEAR YOUR COMPETITORS, HOPING TO SHIFT CUSTOMERS TOWARDS YOUR PRODUCTS AND SERVICES, DESPITE THEM BEING SUBPAR AND MORE EXPENSIVE.

'Change is the law of life. And those who look only to the past or present are certain to miss the future.'

— John F. Kennedy

TURN BACK TIME

DO EVERYTHING POSSIBLE TO DELUDE YOURSELF INTO BELIEVING YOU'RE STILL IN THE COMPANY'S GOLDEN ERA.

WAIT FOR THE NEXT TECH LEAP

WHY INVEST IN, FOR EXAMPLE, DIGITAL COMMUNICATION TOOLS WHEN YOU'RE CERTAIN THAT TELEPATHIC COMMUNICATION IS JUST AROUND THE CORNER?

'PUT PEOPLE FIRST'

YOUR PREFERENCE FOR FACE-TO-FACE MEETINGS, CORRIDOR CHATS, AND HANDWRITTEN MESSAGES STEMS FROM YOUR PHILOSOPHY OF PUTTING PEOPLE BEFORE TECHNOLOGY.

'In any given moment, we have two options: to step forward into growth or to step back into safety.'

— Abraham Maslow

STAND UP FOR HUMANITY

WE'VE SEEN THE MOVIES WHERE THE ROBOTS REBEL. WHY CONTRIBUTE TO HUMANITY'S DOWNFALL BY INVESTING IN ROBOTS AND AI?

'Any change, even a change for the better, is always accompanied by drawbacks and discomforts.'

— Arnold Bennett, English author, 1867-1931

HOW TO RESIST CHANGE
AS AN INDIVIDUAL

BLAME IT ON LACK OF TIME

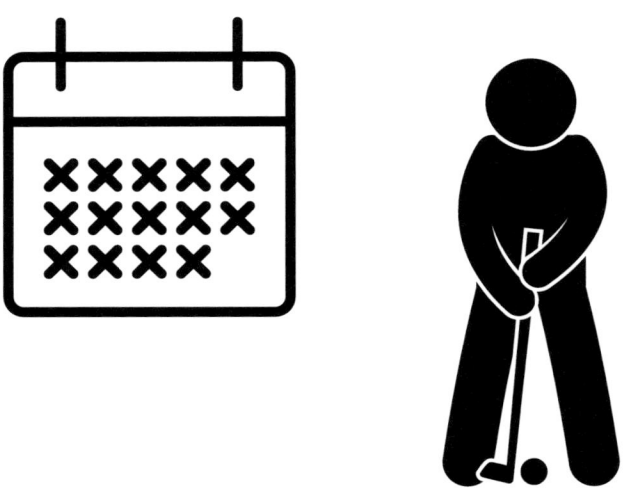

CREATE THE ILLUSION THAT YOU HAVE TOO MUCH TO DO
AND THEREFORE DON'T HAVE TIME TO MAKE CHANGES.

ACT WITH EXAGGERATED PASSION

DISPLAY UNRESTRAINED ENTHUSIASM FOR THE CHANGE.
IT WILL MAKE OTHERS THINK THAT EMPLOYEES ARE BEING
BRAINWASHED AND THEY MIGHT BE NEXT.

CALL OFF MEETINGS YOU'VE SET UP

SCHEDULE MEETINGS WITH KEY INDIVIDUALS DRIVING
THE CHANGE, THEN CANCEL THEM AT THE LAST MOMENT
WITHOUT NOTIFYING THEM.

QUESTION ALL DECISIONS

CHALLENGE EVERY DECISION. IT MAKES YOU SEEM DILIGENT AND RESPONSIBLE, BUT IN REALITY YOU'RE JUST TRYING TO STALL THE CHANGE.

'If you want to make enemies, try to change something.'

— Woodrow Wilson, US president 1913–1921

SABOTAGE COMMUNICATION

ENSURE THAT ALL COMMUNICATION ABOUT THE CHANGE ENCOUNTERS 'TECHNICAL ISSUES'.

SPAM WITH NONSENSICAL CONTENT

USE GENERATIVE AI TO CREATE A CONSTANT STREAM OF TRIVIAL CONTENT AND SPAM EVERYONE INVOLVED IN THE CHANGE PROJECT.

MOCK CHANGE ADVOCATES

SEIZE EVERY CHANCE TO RIDICULE COLLEAGUES WHO OPENLY SUPPORT THE CHANGE.

PRETEND TO CARE ABOUT SECURITY

INSIST ON HALTING ALL CHANGES CITING 'SECURITY REASONS'. FEW WILL ARGUE BACK BECAUSE THEY KNOW SECURITY IS PARAMOUNT.

INVENT FALSE MOTIVES

INVENT FALSE REASONS FOR DECISIONS TO SOW DOUBT AND MISTRUST.

CREATE RESISTANCE GROUPS

FORM INFORMAL GROUPS OPPOSING THE CHANGE TO AMPLIFY RESISTANCE.

SAY ONE THING, DO ANOTHER

APPEAR AGREEABLE AND GIVE THE IMPRESSION THAT YOU'LL MEET EXPECTATIONS, BUT IN TRUTH YOU'RE DOING THE EXACT OPPOSITE.

'The art of life lies in a constant readjustment to our surroundings.'

— Kakuzo Okakaura

BLAME BAD CONDITIONS

EMPHASIZE THE UNFAVORABLE CONDITIONS THAT NECESSITATE HALTING THE CHANGE IMMEDIATELY.

CLAIM A LACK OF RESOURCES

APPROACH THE SITUATION WITH OPTIMISM, BUT EMPHASIZE THE NEED FOR ADDITIONAL RESOURCES. RESOURCES THAT, OF COURSE, ARE NOT READILY AVAILABLE.

INVENT BAD OUTCOMES

If we make changes at the bottom, it will negatively affect the bonus system at the top.

STRESS THE NEED TO REASSESS THE MANAGEMENT'S BONUS SYSTEM BEFORE THE CHANGE. IT WILL HALT THE INITIATIVE.

WITHHOLD INFORMATION

ENSURE THAT ALL PERTINENT INFORMATION YOU POSSESS
FOR THE CHANGE PROJECT REMAINS UNFOUND. FOREVER.

STALL AS MUCH AS POSSIBLE

STALL, STALL, STALL. EXECUTE ALL TASKS AT THE SLOWEST PACE POSSIBLE.

PRESENT IMPOSSIBLE DEMANDS

The project fails to satisfy the requirements outlined in section 28, paragraph 11 of the 'B2-HN-ZE Framework'.

SCOUR THE INTERNET FOR OUTLANDISH CRITERIA THE CHANGE PROJECT CAN'T POSSIBLY MEET, ENSURING IT IS SHUT DOWN.

BE ANNOYING

CHOOSE TO BE ANNOYING TO ANYONE SHOWING EVEN A HINT OF AMBITION ABOUT MAKING THE CHANGE.

START A TROLL FACTORY

ENLIST EVERYONE YOU KNOW TO DISRUPT THE CHANGE INITIATIVE WITH ANONYMOUS POSTS AND COMMENTS ACROSS VARIOUS ONLINE FORUMS.

CUT YOURSELF OFF FROM REALITY

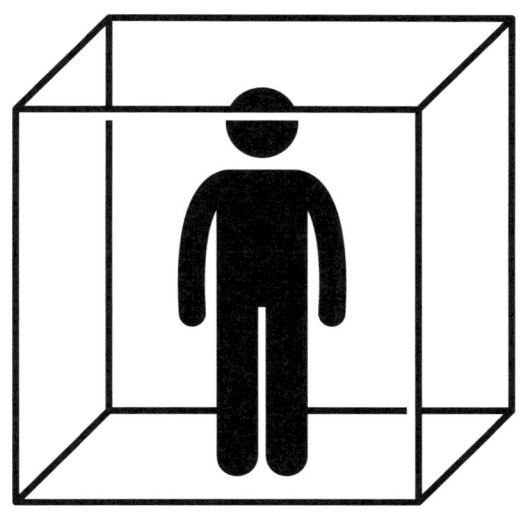

COMPLETELY ISOLATE YOURSELF FROM ANY INTERACTION
WITH REALITY. IN DOING SO, YOU'LL REMAIN UNAWARE OF
ANY CHANGES, ELIMINATING THE NEED TO ADAPT.

MOBILIZE YOUR COLLEAGUES

ACCENTUATE ANY NEGATIVE SENTIMENTS YOUR COLLEAGUES MIGHT HAVE ABOUT THE CHANGE TO GALVANIZE THE RESISTANCE.

PROPOSE A DIFFERENT 'SOLUTION'

OFFER A SOLUTION THAT BY SOME INEXPLICABLE MAGIC,
NECESSITATES NO CHANGE AT ALL.

TAKE IT EASY

CHILL — THE CHANGE ISN'T ABOUT YOU AFTER ALL.

USE THAT PARACHUTE

IF YOU'RE LUCKY ENOUGH TO HAVE A GOLDEN PARACHUTE,
DO EVERYTHING IN YOUR POWER TO BECOME SO
UNDESIRABLE YOU'RE MADE REDUNDANT.

'The greatest discovery of all time is that a person can change his future by merely changing his attitude.'

— Oprah Winfrey

FUEL THE RUMOUR MILL

I heard Bob from Finance has been putting sand in the coffee machine, and he's getting it from Sharon in IT.

SHARE OFFICE GOSSIP TO SOW UNCERTAINTY, FEAR, AND CONFUSION USING ENTIRELY FABRICATED AND UTTERLY BAFFLING RUMORS.

FUEL CONFLICT

FUEL CONFLICT BETWEEN VARIOUS DEPARTMENTS TO OBSTRUCT COLLABORATION AND AGREEMENT ABOUT THE CHANGE.

CONDUCT POINTLESS MEETINGS

Cute cat

INVITE KEY INDIVIDUALS TO POINTLESS MEETINGS WHERE
YOU DELIVER LENGTHY MONOLOGUES ABOUT UTTERLY
IRRELEVANT TOPICS.

SABOTAGE MEETINGS

Sorry for being late, removing the lint from my belly button took more time than expected!

ARRIVE LATE AND UNEXPECTEDLY AT CRUCIAL MEETINGS TO WHICH YOU HAVEN'T BEEN INVITED.

CONTRIBUTE TO MEETING OVERLOAD

SET UP NUMEROUS FICTITIOUS MEETINGS WITHOUT A CLEAR PURPOSE OR AGENDA, ENSURING PARTICIPANTS MISS OUT ON THE GENUINELY NECESSARY AND PRODUCTIVE ONES.

USE MASTER SUPPRESSION TECHNIQUES

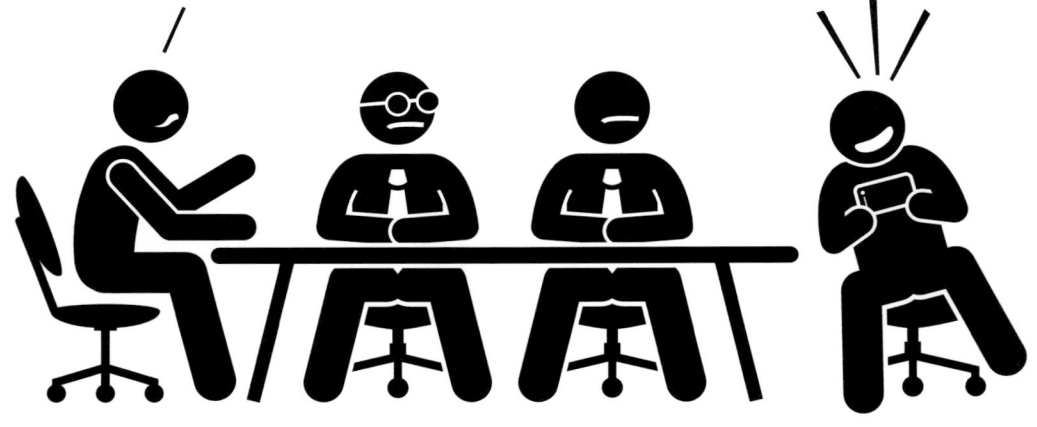

DEPLOY YOUR FULL ARSENAL OF MASTER SUPPRESSION
TECHNIQUES TO INSTILL DOUBT AND ENSURE INACTION.

DESTROY 'SENSITIVE' INFORMATION

ENSURE THAT ANY INFORMATION SUGGESTING A NEED
FOR CHANGE, AND THUS CONSIDERED THREATENING, IS
COMPLETELY ELIMINATED.

CENSOR EVERYTHING

Allow me to assist by submitting the report to the change team, freeing you up to focus on more pressing matters.

VOLUNTEER TO SERVE AS A GO-BETWEEN. THIS ALLOWS YOU TO BLOCK CRUCIAL INFORMATION FROM GETTING TO THE CHANGE TEAM.

LABEL THE CHANGE AS LAME

ARGUE THAT THE CHANGE NEEDS TO BE STOPPED FOR NOT
BEING REVOLUTIONARY OR 'DISRUPTIVE' ENOUGH.

BLAME IT

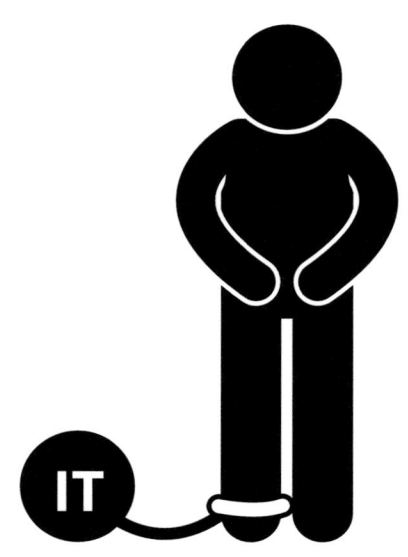

ARGUE THAT CHANGE IS UNFEASIBLE BECAUSE OF ALL YOUR OUTDATED AND RIGID IT SYSTEMS, WHICH ARE, OF COURSE, IRREPLACEABLE.

DEMOTIVATE THE CHANGE AGENTS

To be honest, our progress up to this point is entirely due to my efforts.

TAKE CREDIT FOR THE IDEAS OF THE CHANGE AGENTS, DEMORALISING THEM SO MUCH THEY WON'T PURSUE THE TRANSFORMATION FURTHER.

'Change is hard because people overestimate the value of what they have and underestimate the value of what they may gain by giving that up.'

— James Belasco & Ralph Stayer, 1994

HIDE IN PLAIN SIGHT

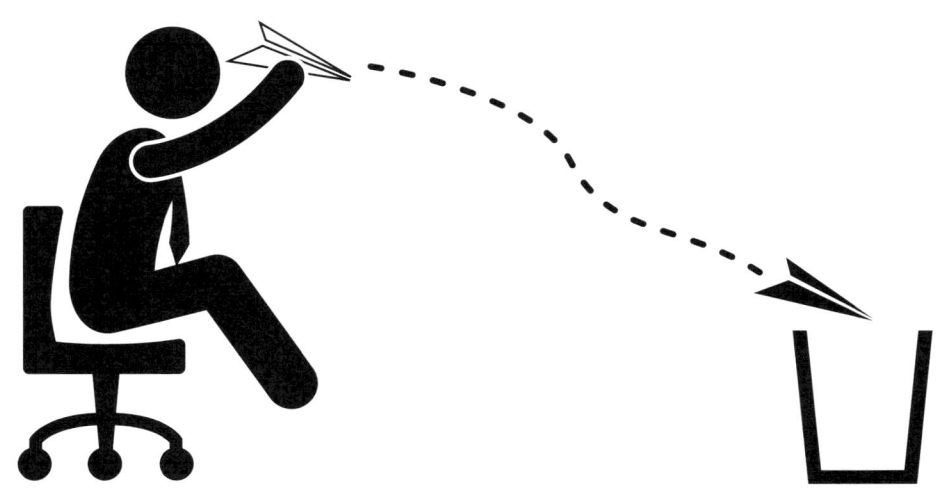

PERFORM TASKS THAT ARE SO TRIVIAL AND WASTEFUL THAT THEY, AND CONSEQUENTLY YOU, ARE OVERLOOKED.

OUTSOURCE YOUR JOB TO AI

DELEGATE YOUR TASKS TO AI, ALLOWING YOU TO DISENGAGE
FROM WORKPLACE CONCERNS AND EARN A PASSIVE INCOME.

MAKE YOURSELF INDISPENSABLE

ASSERT THAT YOU'VE DEVELOPED A CRUCIAL BUSINESS SYSTEM USING COMPLEX SPAGHETTI CODE, MAKING YOU INDISPENSABLE TO THE COMPANY'S ONGOING OPERATIONS.

WHEN NOTHING ELSE WORKS

BLAME IT ON BAD WIFI

BLAME IT ON POOR WIFI. IT'S A UNIVERSAL EXCUSE.

INVENT AN ALTERNATE REALITY

EXPLORE VARIOUS WAYS OF ESCAPING REALITY, LIKE
CRAFTING YOUR OWN ALTERNATE UNIVERSE.

BECOME INVISIBLE

GO UNDER THE RADAR AND SET UP TIME-CONSUMING DISTRACTIONS.

ENTERTAIN EVIL THOUGHTS

WISH LONG AND HARD FOR SOMETHING TERRIBLE TO HAPPEN THAT PUTS A STOP TO THE CHANGE.

USE YOUR MIND POWER

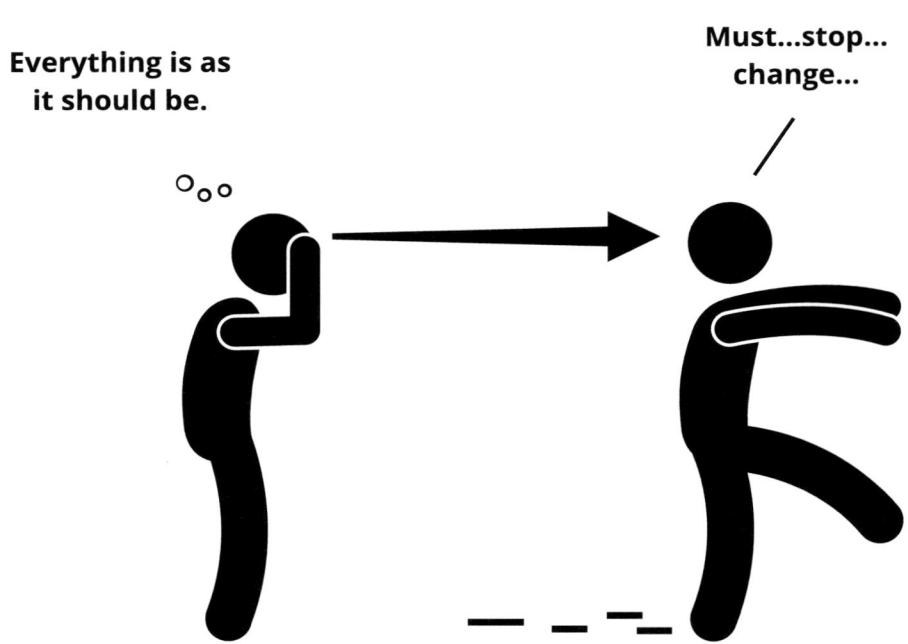

MASTER THE ART OF INFLUENCING OTHERS WITH YOUR
THOUGHTS TO ENSURE THEY ALIGN WITH YOUR
'NO CHANGE' AGENDA.

PULL THE PLUG

IF NOTHING ELSE WORKS, PULL THE PLUG ON THE CHANGE PROJECT.

'Times and conditions change so rapidly that we must keep our aim constantly focused on the future.'

— Walt Disney